A first guide to

◆

The USA

By Kath Davies

A ZOË BOOK

A ZOË BOOK

© 1995 Zoë Books Limited

Devised and produced by
Zoë Books Limited
15 Worthy Lane
Winchester
Hampshire SO23 7AB
England

Illustrative material used in this book first appeared in *Discovering The U.S.A.*, published by Zoë Books Limited.

First published in Great Britain in 1995 by
Zoë Books Limited
15 Worthy Lane
Winchester
Hampshire SO23 7AB

A record of the CIP data is available from the British Library.

ISBN 1 874488 39 8

Printed in Italy by Grafedit SpA
Design: Jan Sterling, Sterling Associates
Editor: Denise Allard
Picture research: Victoria Sturgess
Map: Gecko Limited
Production: Grahame Griffiths

Photographic acknowledgments

The publishers wish to acknowledge, with thanks, the following photographic sources:

Cover: Robert Harding Picture Library; title page: Zefa; 5l&r,6 Robert Harding Picture Library; 7l Frank Sloan; 7r,8,9l&r Robert Harding Picture Library; 10 Impact Photos/Alain le Garsmeur; 11l Frank Sloan; 11r Robert Harding Picture Library; 12 Zefa; 13l&r Robert Harding Picture Library; 14 Impact Photos/Alastair Indge; 15l Frank Sloan; 15r The Hutchison Library/Liba Taylor; 16 Wayne Schwaeber; 17l Zefa; 17r Karen Pandell; 18,19l Zefa; 19r The Hutchison Library/Liba Taylor; 20, 21l Robert Harding Picture Library; 21r Zefa; 22 Allsport/Rick Stewart; 23l The Hutchison Library/Robert Francis; 23r,24 Robert Harding Picture Library; 25l&r Frank Sloan; 26 Robert Harding Picture Library; 27l National Gallery, Washington D.C.; 27r Hulton Deutsch Collection/The Bettmann Archive; 28 Hulton Deutsch Collection; 29l Peter Newark's Western Americana; 29r NASA

Cover: *Children in New York*

Title page: *US flags, on 4th July, Independence Day*

Contents

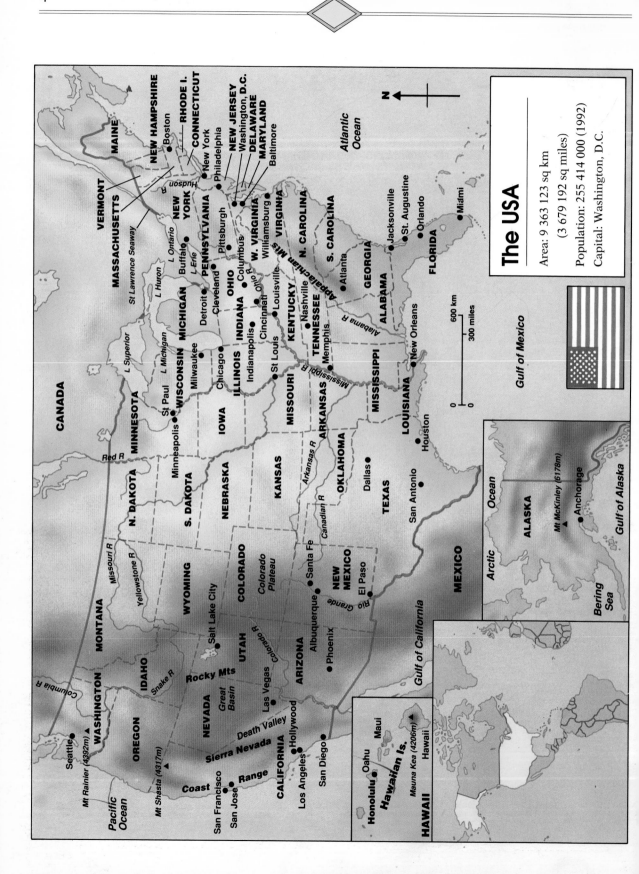

The USA

Area: 9 363 123 sq km
(3 679 192 sq miles)
Population: 255 414 000 (1992)
Capital: Washington, D.C.

Welcome to the USA!

The United States of America stretch across the land from the Pacific Ocean to the Atlantic Ocean. The country is made up of 50 states. The state of Alaska is in the far north, towards the Arctic Ocean. The islands of Hawaii are to the west, in the Pacific Ocean.

Most people live and work in towns and cities. There are not many people in the wild areas of the country. There are great forests, grasslands or prairies, swamps, deserts and mountains in the USA.

▼ A truck on a country road

▲ Native Americans, New Mexico

The people

The first Native Americans came from Asia, about 50 000 years ago.

People from Europe probably arrived about 1000 years ago. Dutch, Spanish, French and British settlers landed about 500 years ago. Many Africans were brought to work as slaves.

Since then, people have come to live in the USA from all over the world. They have different languages, faiths and customs, but they are all US citizens.

Around the Northeast

Six states make up the region of New England. They are Maine, Rhode Island, New Hampshire, Vermont, Connecticut and Massachusetts.

New England's name comes from its first settlers. These people arrived from England in 1620. They were Christians, who wanted to worship in their own way. They were known as 'Pilgrims'. The pilgrims' first town was Boston, which is now an industrial city.

New England is a beautiful area. The trees on the low hills turn red, orange and gold in September. Cape Cod, on the rocky Atlantic coast, is named after the fish in the sea there.

▼ The 'Stars and Stripes' fly outside a house in Vermont

New York, New York

About 350 years ago, Dutch settlers came to live in the Hudson Valley. This area was later ruled by Britain and became known as New York.

New York City has been a gateway to the USA for millions of people. The Statue of Liberty stands on an island in the harbour.

Today more than 7 million people live in New York City. It is the largest city in the USA. At its heart is the island of

▲ The Statue of Liberty

Manhattan. Here, tall new skyscrapers overshadow the old buildings. New York is a centre of trade, music, art, opera and dance. Theatres line the famous street called Broadway.

▼ The Empire State Building, New York

Atlantic states

The states of New Jersey, Delaware and Pennsylvania lie on the Atlantic coast. The state capital of Pennsylvania is Philadelphia. When America broke away from Britain's rule in 1776, the Declaration of Independence was signed here.

The capital city

Washington, in the District of Columbia, is the capital city of the USA. It is named after George Washington (1732-1799), who was the first President of the United States.

Washington is a city of fine buildings, wide streets, parks and gardens. Members of the US Congress, part of the government, meet in the Capitol building. The official home of the President is the White House, which was built in the 1790s. Some of the houses in the city's Georgetown area are also about 200 years old.

▲ The Capitol Building, Washington D.C.

Politics and presidents

People in the USA choose their government. This way of governing is called a democracy. The people vote for the members of the Senate and the House of Representatives. These two parts of government make up the US Congress. Congress makes the laws of the country.

The two main political parties in the USA are the Democrats and the Republicans. Each party decides on the person they would like to become the President, and the people of the USA then vote. The President is the Head of State, and serves for four years.

▼ A street in Georgetown

▲ President Abraham Lincoln

Sights to see

The Washington Monument was finished in 1884. It is a very tall stone pillar.

The Lincoln Memorial is a building which contains a statue of Abraham Lincoln (1809-1865). He was the 16th President of the USA.

The National Gallery has some of the world's finest paintings.

Rare animals and plants are kept in the Zoo and the Botanical Garden. People go to see them and to study them.

The Library of Congress contains a copy of every book which is published in the USA.

The South

The southern states are West Virginia, Virginia, Maryland, Kentucky, Tennessee, North and South Carolina, Georgia, Florida, Alabama and Mississippi.

▲ Horses race in the Kentucky Derby

In the 1860s, most of the workers on the large farms, or plantations, in the south were slaves. They were brought to the USA by ship from Africa. The northern states wanted to end slavery, but the south did not. The southern states then tried to break away from the north. This led to the outbreak of the American Civil War, which the north won in 1865.

▲ Old and new buildings, Atlanta

Visiting the south

Many people come to walk in the Appalachian Mountains in Virginia. They may also visit the town of Williamsburg. There they can see fine old buildings from the time of the first settlers in the 1600s.

Kentucky is famous for its racehorses. The world's largest underground caves are in Kentucky. They are the Mammoth Caves, which together stretch for 500 kilometres (310 miles).

People of all ages visit Orlando in Florida to see Disney World.

Business

People in the south work in modern businesses such as the computer industry.

Atlanta, in Georgia, is a fast-growing city. Its airport, Hartsfield, is the third busiest in the USA. At Cape Canaveral in Florida, the US space flights are launched.

The Everglades

The weather in the far south is warm. Florida's Everglades form a large wetland area. Alligators, rare birds and snakes live here. There are about 500 National Wildlife Refuges in the USA.

▼ An alligator in the Everglades

West of the Mississippi

The south-central states of the USA are Louisiana, Arkansas, Missouri, Kansas, Oklahoma, Texas, New Mexico and Colorado.

About 300 years ago, French and Spanish people explored the valleys of the two great rivers, the Mississippi and the Missouri. The centre of the old city of New Orleans still has a French style.

The Mississippi River flows south to the Gulf of Mexico. It is joined by the Missouri and the Ohio rivers. This is the biggest river system in the USA, running for 3745 kilometres (2322 miles).

▼ A jazz band plays in New Orleans

▲ A cattle round-up, New Mexico

There are hot water springs in Arkansas. The Native Americans and the Spanish used them to heal sick people. The springs are still used today. To the west lie the farms and prairies of Kansas and Oklahoma, and the cattle lands of Texas.

The legend of the Alamo

Texas was once part of Mexico, and was ruled by Spain. In 1836 a small band of Texans, led by Davy Crockett, fought against the Spanish at a place called Alamo (now in the city of San Antonio). There are songs and stories about the bravery of those fighters.

Plains and mountains

The state of Texas is a huge, dry plain. Cattle farms and oil wells have made the state grow rich. Now the cities of Texas are centres of industry. Dallas, Houston and San Antonio are among the largest US cities.

In the limestone rocks of New Mexico there are the famous Carlsbad Caverns. Millions of bats live in these caves.

The Rocky Mountains stretch across Colorado state. In the 1850s, miners came here to search for gold. Now visitors enjoy skiing and hiking in the mountains.

▼ A ski-lift in Colorado

Lakes and prairies

The north-central states include Ohio, Iowa, Indiana, Illinois, Michigan, Wisconsin, North and South Dakota, Minnesota and Nebraska.

▲ The waterfront, Detroit

The Great Lakes reach across some of these states. Together they form the largest area of fresh water in the world. The five lakes are Erie, Ontario, Huron, Michigan and Superior. The first European settlers used the lakes to carry goods inland. Today, the St Lawrence Seaway runs along the USA's border with Canada. It links the Great Lakes with the Atlantic Ocean.

▲ The Sears Tower, Chicago

'Motown'

Detroit, in the state of Michigan, is the home of the US motor industry. It was nicknamed 'Motown'. The most famous US car maker, Henry Ford (1863-1947), came from near Detroit.

About 60 years ago, Ford set up Greenfield Village. It is a museum where the workshops of inventors have been rebuilt.

Chicago

Almost 3 million people live in Chicago, Illinois. It is the third largest city in the USA. It is known as the 'windy city' because of the prairie winds.

The Sears Tower, in Chicago, is the world's tallest building. It is 443 metres (1486 feet) high, and has 110 storeys.

Into the country

The midwestern states are called the 'Corn Belt'. This is where the USA's huge grain crops are grown. Wisconsin is noted for dairy farming. South Dakota is famous for its beautiful Black Hills.

▼ Cornfields in Iowa

The Wild West

The far west of the USA lies beyond the Rocky Mountains. Yellowstone is the oldest National Park in the USA. It is on the borders of the mountain states of Idaho, Montana and Wyoming. The park is famous for its grizzly bears, and for its natural springs, or geysers.

The states of Utah, Nevada and Arizona are desert areas. In Utah there are rocks which the weather has worn away into strange shapes and deep canyons. The Grand Canyon in Arizona is the deepest in the world. It is 443 kilometres (275 miles) long and 1.5 kilometres (1 mile) deep.

▼ The Grand Canyon, seen from a helicopter

▲ Surfers in California

Western cities

Las Vegas, in Nevada, has many gambling casinos. Its bright lights shine out over the desert. Salt Lake City, in Utah, was built by religious people called Mormons in 1847. Phoenix, Arizona, is an industrial city.

The West Coast

The states of Washington and Oregon have cool, wet weather. There are lakes and forests in this north western area. Many people visit the beautiful park in the Yosemite Valley.

California runs down the Pacific coast to the border of Mexico and has a warm climate. The largest trees on earth, the giant sequoias, grow here.

More than 3 million people live in Los Angeles, where Hollywood is the centre of the film industry.

Ice and fire

Alaska is mostly a wilderness of forest and ice. The Aleut and the Inuit peoples live there.

Hawaii's warm islands are the tops of volcanoes. Some of these volcanoes still erupt with boiling streams of lava.

▼ Ice and lakes in Alaska

Everyday life

Most people in the USA used to work on the land or in factories. Now machines do many of these jobs. People work with computers and in electronics industries. They also work in banks, businesses, hotels and shops. These are called service industries.

▲ A car factory in Detroit

People go to work for about eight hours every day. Holidays are shorter in the USA than they are in Europe. However, there are not enough jobs for everyone. Visitors are often surprised by the number of poor people they see on the streets.

▲ Loyalty to the USA

Housing and homes

Many families live in their own houses. However, more and more people, especially in big cities, live in flats in large buildings. These flats are often rented, not owned.

Freedom to believe

There is no official religion in the USA. People are free to choose any faith, or none. More than half of the people are Christians. There are about 6 million Jewish people and 6 million Muslims in the USA.

Going to school

Education is free in the USA. There are also private schools where parents pay to send their children. The school day starts at about 8 am and ends at 3 pm. After school there are sports clubs and other activities.

Most children attend school from the ages of 5 to 16. They transfer to 'High School' when they are 12 or 13. When they reach 16, they can go on to college or they can go to work.

▼ Reading the Jewish Torah

Food in the USA

The cookery of many different countries, such as Italy, Spain, China and Japan, can be found in the USA. People often like food to be tasty, cheap and fast! Chains of fast-food restaurants serve hot dogs, chicken, pizzas, hamburgers and salads. This food can also be taken away to eat at home.

In cities, supermarkets and shops may stay open 24 hours a day. There are also bakers, butchers and open-air markets which sell fresh bread, meat, fruit and vegetables. In country areas, people can buy food straight from the farms, as well as in shops in the small towns.

▼ Buying a meal to take away

Around the states

Many regions produce their own special food and drinks.

New England is famous for its seafood, such as lobsters or clam chowder (stew). Boston is the home of baked beans.

Maryland is known for its crabs and oysters, and Kentucky fried chicken is famous around the world.

Texas beef is often cooked on barbecues. 'Tex-Mex' mixes Texan and Mexican dishes.

Louisiana has spicy shrimps and a fish stew called 'gumbo'.

California is famous for wines.

▼ Food for a street party

▲ A crab dish from the south

Thanksgiving dinner

On the fourth Thursday in November, Americans take a holiday. Families and friends eat a special meal together. It is called a Thanksgiving dinner. People remember the early settlers who came to New England about 375 years ago. They gave thanks for their first year in America. Like the settlers, Americans today eat turkey, cranberry sauce and pumpkin pie for Thanksgiving.

Sports for everyone

People enjoy playing and watching all sorts of sports. Many large cities in the USA have famous football and baseball teams. There are also ice hockey, basketball and tennis teams. The huge sports grounds are packed with crowds of cheering fans.

▼ The Dallas Cowboys and the Buffalo Bills in the Super Bowl

▲ Volleyball in New York City

Many city teams have names, such as the Boston Red Sox, or the Chicago Bears. Some of the players are as famous, and as rich, as film stars.

The Super Bowl is a football match which is held in January. The winning teams in the two American football divisions play each other. The World Series is a set, or series, of baseball games. Volleyball is also very popular. Millions of people watch these games on television. Many people play in their own local teams.

Out of doors

Tennis, golf and squash are popular sports. People also keep fit by running and jogging.

Tourists visit the coast and the countryside. They walk, swim, sail and water-ski. Canoeing and rafting are also popular. Surfers go to California and Hawaii for the high waves.

Many children go to summer camp. They are taught sports such as tennis, or swimming, and they go on long walks.

Climbers go to the rocky peaks in Colorado or Yosemite.

Winter sports include skiing and skating.

▼ On the trail in Wyoming

Arts and entertainment

Many cities in the USA have theatres, orchestras, dance and opera companies. People from other countries have brought their own music and dances to America. In turn, the music of the USA has travelled to many lands. Jazz, blues, country, folk, rock and rap have fans around the world.

▼ A film set for a 'Wild West' film

Classical music, ballet and modern dance are popular. Cinema and television have shown life in the USA to the rest of the world. Now many people watch films on video in their own homes.

Art and architecture

The Native American people made beautiful jewellery, pottery and carvings. The first settlers made fine beds, chairs and tables for their homes. They painted the countryside and its animals and birds. They also made pictures of their new homes and their families.

▼ Sculpture by Alexander Calder

▲ A bookstall in New York City

The tall skyscrapers of the cities led the way in modern architecture. Many famous art galleries are in the USA.

Writing

Mark Twain wrote children's books such as *Huckleberry Finn*. Other children's favourites include *What Katy Did*, by Susan Coolidge. Some popular children's writers of today are Judy Blume, Rosa Guy, Maurice Sendak and Randall Jarrell.

Adults enjoy the plays of Tennessee Williams and Lillian Hellman, and the novels of Alice Walker and Saul Bellow.

A long time ago

Between 60 000 and 10 000 years ago, the climate changed many times. The sea level dropped, and hunters could walk across from what is now Siberia into North America.

Over thousands of years, people moved across the land. They learned to farm, and grew beans, corn and other crops. People today have found the things which they made.

The first Europeans who sailed to North America, about 1000 years ago, were probably the Vikings.

▼ These buildings at Mesa Verde, in Colorado, are more than 1000 years old.

▲ President George Washington

Wars with Britain

British people in the US had to pay taxes to Britain, but they had no Members of Parliament.

The people thought this was not a fair way to govern. They signed a Declaration of Independence in 1776. Then they fought Britain, and won. The leaders wrote down how they wanted to be governed. It was the first US Constitution. In 1789 the leaders elected George Washington to be the first President of the United States of America.

A growing country

During the last 150 years, people have spread across North America. They moved south and west. They have cut down forests and built railways across the land.

Miners moved west to find gold in California and Colorado. Farmers and ranchers began to settle on the lands where the Native American people lived and hunted buffalo.

After many wars, the Native American peoples were made to live in special areas called reservations.

The Civil War (1861-65) ended in a victory for the northern states. It ended slavery for African Americans.

▼ Foot soldiers in the south

The new country

About 100 years ago, there was work for everyone who wanted it in the USA. More and more people arrived from countries such as Italy, eastern Europe and China. They all hoped for a better life in the USA.

▲ Film star Bob Hope visited US soldiers in Britain during the Second World War.

Some people's lives were in danger in their own countries. They wanted to follow their own faiths, or they disagreed with the way in which their country was ruled. Many people found that life was hard in the USA too. They had to work for very low wages. However, some families did grow rich.

▲ Waiting for cheap food, 1931

War and peace

The USA fought with Britain and France against Germany during the First World War (1914-1918). After the war, there was a time called the Depression, when many people had no work.

In 1941 the USA joined in the Second World War. This war ended in 1945. After the war, the USA and the Soviet Union became enemies. This time was called the 'Cold War', because there was no fighting.

Two of the USA's most famous leaders were killed in the 1960s. President John F Kennedy and Dr Martin Luther King, who worked for black Americans' civil rights, were both shot.

In spite of these troubles, the people of the USA have worked to make the US one of the richest and strongest countries in the world.

▼ On the Moon, 1973

30

Fact file

Government

The US President and the Vice-President are chosen, or elected, every four years. The Senate has two members for every state. Senators are elected to serve for six years. The House of Representatives has 435 members. They are elected every two years. The number of members for each state depends on the number of people who live in the state.

Flag

The US flag is called the 'stars and stripes'. The stars stand for the 50 states.

National anthem

The national song, or anthem, of the USA was written by Francis Scott Key in 1812. The name of the anthem is *The Star-Spangled Banner*. It is played on many special occasions.

National emblem

The national badge, or emblem, of the USA is the bald eagle. Most of these birds live in Alaska, but there are a few in other states now.

Money

Money in the USA is made up of dollars and cents. There are 100 cents in one dollar. The five-cent coin is called a nickel, and the 10-cent coin is a dime. A quarter is 25 cents, and a half-dollar is 50 cents. The notes which are used every day are for amounts of $1, $5, $10, $20, $50 and $100.

Holidays and festivals

Holidays include:

Independence Day (4 July), Labor Day (1st Monday in September), Thanksgiving (4th Thursday in November), Christmas Day (25 December) and New Year's Day (1 January).

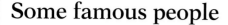

Some famous people

Pocahontas (c.1595-1617) was a Native American woman.

Eli Whitney (1765-1825) invented a machine to clean cotton, called a cotton gin.

John James Audubon (1785-1851) was a wildlife artist.

Emily Dickinson (1830-66) was one of the USA's greatest poets.

Sitting Bull (c.1831-90) was a Native American leader.

Thomas Edison (1847-1931) invented the light bulb and the gramophone.

Amelia Earhart (1897-1937) was the first woman to fly across the Atlantic Ocean.

Louis Armstrong (1900-71) was a great jazz musician.

Walt Disney (1901-66) was a film cartoonist, or animator.

Jesse Owens (1913-80) was an Olympic athlete. *Lincoln*

Toni Morrison (1931-) won the Nobel Prize for literature.

Some key events in history

1513: the Spanish landed in Florida.

1607: a British colony was set up at Jamestown, Virginia.

1625: the Dutch founded New Amsterdam, later New York.

1763: the British ruled in North America.

1775-81: the American War of Independence.

1849: Gold Rush in California.

1861-65: American Civil War

1890: the wars with the Native Americans ended.

1917: the USA entered the First World War.

1920: women allowed to vote.

1929: the Great Depression.

1941: the USA entered the Second World War.

1963: President John F Kennedy *were* was assassinated.

1969: US astronauts landed on the moon.

Index